Everything My Parents Taught Me in 6 Easy Steps:

A Life's Guide

Shelby Davis, MS

Copy Editing:

Right House Publications™

Published: *December 25th, 2018*

Author: *Shelby Davis*

Head Editing: *Shelby Davis*

Project Assistant Editors: *Nick Gambacini and Emily Sirko*

All Rights Reserved.

Note: All names in this book have been changed to protect the identities of those involved.

Foreword

From a young age, my parents sought to instill in me a certain series of values and lessons with which I credit my accomplishments and my ability to set and realize goals. Over time I have compiled these life lessons, and I came to realize it was time for me to share them with my students. As a public school counselor for seven years, I have worked directly with students to help them with a diverse range of situations, including overcoming chronic absenteeism, bettering self-awareness, and strengthening mental health, as well as offering assistance with career vocational planning, relationships, and personal life goals. I have always had a passion for helping others, and I believe that my life experiences, thus far, have put me in a position to be of service.

In 2014, while attending a conference for counselors in Orlando, Florida, I came up with the idea to create a textual guide that students could carry around with them for motivation and advice. I remember my days in high school when I was confused about many things in life, from selecting a college, to taking the time to understand what I wanted my life to be. My hope is that by the end of this book, you are not only better equipped to tackle life's daily difficulties, but are inspired with the courage to realize your full potential, for as former British Prime Minister Winston Churchill said, "To improve is to change; to be perfect is to change often".

Behold! This is everything my parents taught me in six easy steps...

Go Forward.

Shelby

Acknowledgments

FIRST AND FOREMOST, I have unending gratitude for my parents, Mr. Rodney and Mrs. Pamela Davis. I would also like to thank Michele Pilver, Tara Travasano, Michael Wilson, Stefanie Wilson, Andrey Masser, Gennifer Dorgan, Cheryl Newland, Tyler Collodel, Nicholas Gambacini, and Julian Adorno.

~

TO MY WONDERFUL PARENTS

Table of Contents

"You see us as you want to see us - in the simplest terms, in the most convenient definitions. But what we found is that each one of us is a brain... and an athlete... and a basket case...a princess... and a criminal. Does that answer your question?"

– Bender, *The Breakfast Club*

Step One: Set a Goal

From a young boy to a teenager, my parents continually taught me of the importance of setting goals. We set goals from, "What do we want to be when we grow up?" to, "What is our purpose in life?" to, "Where are we going?" It all begins with setting a goal. The importance of this first step is described well by motivational speaker, Tony Robbins: "Setting goals is the first step in turning the invisible into the visible." Setting goals in life is very important, whether it is to lose a few pounds, obtain a college degree, or land a career of choice. Goals should push your comfort zone, and college is a great place to do this. Your goals should both be realistic and "unrealistic". Setting a goal is a proactive technique, versus a reactive technique. Proactive means making decisions in advance to optimize your future or career success. Reactive means waiting until problems emerge before stepping in to resolve them. I identify best as a proactive person.

Goals ultimately create your path. A good way to begin work on your goals is to create a list. The best type of list is a chronological list, which ranges from short-term goal to long-term goal, or you can use a priority goal list, which ranges from the most important goal to the least important. As you accomplish your goals, cross them off your list. Please remember not to overwhelm yourself (or exhaust your brain) with a long list. Try beginning with a shorter list, and then adding more goals as you accomplish them (this is ideal for first-time goal setters). Goals should also be practical. For example, "I want to improve my grades this year" versus, "I want to cure cancer" (semi-"unrealistic", but you can achieve all ☺). A good goal should stretch you, but be sure to add a dose of common sense. Go right up to the edge of your comfort zone and then step over it.

Every goal should involve a deadline time and a date. You will need to think about when you plan to achieve that goal. It could be by year-end, for example December 31, or it could be more near-term, such as four months. Without a date, a goal is just a dream and not a reality. Make sure that every goal has and ends with a date of completion. When I was in high school, my goals were to go to college and become a teacher. That was the path I chose. I knew from a young age that I wanted to be in the helping field; although only my mother went to college, I wanted to be an educator, and college was my obvious option. While in college I learned more about the importance of successfully meeting deadlines and dates. I also realized the importance of not missing or pushing something off. Being on schedule or ahead of schedule was one of the many values I obtained from my mother. During my second year of college, I made a slight detour in this path to achieving my goals. Although my goal did not end where I first planned – in the field of Education – I ended up in the related field of Social Work. I always knew I wanted to help those who could not help themselves. It is essential to understand that goals don't have one simple road or path, but many turns and hurdles. Please note it is okay for your path to take twists and turns. That's the nature of life.

A short-term goal is something you want to do in the near future. This can mean today, this week, this month, or even this year; it is something you want to accomplish soon. One short-term goal of mine was to have better control of my finances as my income increases. A budget is a good idea. Having set the goal to have better control of my finances allowed me to be able to have extra spending money and afford my living expenses. Goals are your destination. For example, when you buy a plane ticket, consider that you setting a goal, or the path. When you arrive at your destination, consider that as you reaching your goal. During the travels on your path, you must remember it may feel difficult at times. You also must remember everyone's paths are different; one may reach their goal faster or slower than another. Do not compare your path to others. I encourage you to build and walk down your own path. In addition, some goals may be more challenging than others, such as buying a luxury vehicle versus attaining a part-time job.

Since I began in the field of education, I have encountered numerous individuals with multiple life struggles, trials and tribulations, and goals. However, there is one student who has stood out to me the most. Tyler was a student of mine who is an individual of endurance and motivation. Tyler was diagnosed with Tourettes at a young age, yet never allowed this to deter him from his goals. In addition to this diagnosis, Tyler grew up in a home where his parents were divorced. He had two choices in his early life: be miserable about these challenges and turn into someone that he wouldn't be happy with, or stay active and be positive so that he could grow up, achieve his goals, and be someone that he is proud of. He overcame his obstacles to accomplish his short-term goals to be the person who he intended to be. He was both a high school and college basketball athlete.

It was actor and former Governor Arnold Schwarzenegger who once said, "Strength does not come from winning. Your struggles develop your strengths. When you go through hardships and decide not to surrender, that is strength." Tyler identified his struggles and invested in overcoming them in order to achieve his goals.

Finding my strengths is what my parents instilled in me. They empowered me to understand and find the good qualities I possess. My parents wanted me to frequently use my strengths. I invite you to do the same. My parents helped prepare me for success by providing the background and motivation to reach my goals. Like me, Tyler had a plan and path he would take to achieve his goals for future career and success.

To review step one, there are two major types of goals you can set: long-term or short-term. A long-term goal is something you want to accomplish in the future or something that will take you a long time to accomplish. Long-term goals require time and planning. They are not something you can do this week or even this year. Remember short-term goals are achievable in the near future, for example a few weeks or months, while long-term goals are usually at least years away. It is best to have a potential time frame with your goals, for example one to two years, and so on. Obtaining your goals is not extremely easy, as my parents often reminded me. I encourage you to overcome the bumps and turns in order to obtain your goal. A Quote from the song "Happy Talk" from the musical "South Pacific" said, "If you don't have a dream, How you gonna have a dream come true?" My goal in life was to help others, to be a guiding light. Because of the values I learned from my parents, it has changed my attitude over the years allowing me to achieve the goals I have set.

Step Two: Be Educated (and Go On!)

Continuing on, our next step, number two, is to be educated! From an early age, my parents and I always discussed obtaining higher education. My mother was my only parent who graduated from college. While I've been in the school system, I have worked with some students who told me they didn't need any further education past high school! In reply, I would encourage them to continue their education past high school, which in return would result in a slew of benefits. Those benefits may include increased job opportunities and overall knowledge. There are many avenues you can pursue to further your education. You may attend a traditional university or community college. You can also enroll in a certification program, or you can learn a trade.

Did you know adults who graduated from a four-year college, on average, earn $20,000 more a year as a result of having gotten that degree? (Author, 2014) That means adults who did not attend college on average earned $20,000 a year less (that's fewer times to eat out, buy shoes, and play video games!). Who doesn't mind a little extra money in their pocket?! In a recent research study, surveys conducted both online and over the phone to a diverse population found those who attended higher education were more financially stable than those who didn't. The survey was done in association with the *Chronicle of Higher Education*, and included 1,055 two-year and four-year private, public, and for-profit colleges and universities. This study found that college is worth the time, money, and effort.

If you are ever in doubt, ask yourself what it means to be educated. To answer that question, write down your thoughts and goals.

It should look something like this:

1. To make more money.

2. For better career opportunities

3. Health Benefits!

What is the purpose of education? In essence, I see it as the means to a productive career, not an end in itself. To be educated means to have the knowledge needed to satisfy one's own needs as a human being by engaging in self-sustaining, self-generated action as a productive member of a free society. With an education, you have the opportunities to choose a career versus being narrowed into "dead-end" jobs. Imagine waking up each morning to work in a job field you enjoy, where you have no discomfort about going in. We all know higher education costs money (lots of it), however, think about the possible rewards of higher education. In addition, there are several ways to deal with these high costs, such as financial aid, grants, and scholarships. Having achieved a master's degree in

Counseling and a bachelor's degree in Social Work, I am blessed with having a high-quality level of employment. Having a degree has enabled me to have higher level job with good hours. I am fortunate to be out of work by three o'clock, never work on holidays, have summers off, and retain good health and dental benefits. I appreciate how having an education has allowed me to enjoy these benefits. Without my education, careers with these benefits would not be available to me. I am extremely grateful for these opportunities, and want you to feel this way too!

If you feel college is not right for you, you might consider joining a branch of the service. There are several options you can choose from: the Army, Marines, Coast Guard, and Army Reserve. Having lived my life with family and friends who are in the services, I have witnessed several benefits offered by the armed services. My oldest brother served our country for many years in the Army

Reserve, and it is because of him I saw firsthand how the Military can shape an individual for a quality life. In addition, the benefits of the Navy include competitive pay, health care, tax benefits, college tuition, and the ability to travel the world. However, as the services may be a great option, it is important to remember you must be eligible to enroll.

Although education or higher learning may feel like a waste to some individuals, the benefits are real; increased options to obtaining a career of your choice and learning are the greatest benefit of them all. Give it a try! You can do it!

Step Three: Stay Motivated

The next step, step three, is to ***stay motivated.*** This is one of the hardest tasks or steps for me personally. Life often heavily interferes with this step. Begin by asking yourself whether you are an extrinsically or an intrinsically motivated individual. What does this mean you ask? Extrinsic motivation is when one is motivated to perform a behavior or engage in an activity to earn an external reward or avoid punishment. Intrinsic motivation is the opposite: one is personally rewarded for his or her own sake rather than the desire for an external reward. I remember one morning I dedicated a whole lesson on motivation for my college students. I wanted them to understand what it means to be motivated and which characteristic type best fit them. In the first minute of class, I told them they were all motivated, simply because they were in college working on a goal. I wanted them to know that motivation lies deep inside all of them; they just needed to unleash it.

Inventor Thomas Edison once said, "Our greatest weakness lies in giving up. The most certain way to succeed is always to try just one more time." Don't allow stress to overcome you and make you give up. I can recall many times I wanted to throw in the towel, both in my employment, educational studies, and in life. A few times I wanted to give up on my master's degree and not complete my thesis. However, I knew my parents instilled the strengths in me to carry on and never give up. I learned how to avoid distractions and focus on what was important. I always found my parents to be a strong empowering factor of my life. I found the best way to defeat a negative thought or comment is to take away its power by not giving it your attention. Take back your power. I went through the six steps my parents instilled in me on a regular basis. I knew I had to keep moving along if I wanted to reach my goal. Life is tough and you must stay motivated if you want to achieve your goals. Whatever it takes for you to stay motivated, do it! I always had a love of theater, but I was also scared to audition because I felt I was not good enough. I was a poor singer and most auditions that interested me required singing. I knew that if I really wanted to be a part of a production, I had to stay motivated for my audition. I needed to take steps to overcome my fear and go for what I wanted. I had to overcome my fear of auditions. I practiced achieving what I wanted. I showed up for auditions and did the best I could. I faced my fear and overcame my anxiety. Now today I have been part of over 50 productions.

From my personal experiences, I had down days where I was pessimistic and tended to see only the worst. However, I had to remember my reason for taking on the task at hand. I stayed motivated because I had a desire to complete the task or achieve my goal. I also trained my mind to think positive. Negative thinking only breeds more negativity. It is a happiness riptide. It will carry you away from shore and if you don't swim away from it, will pull you under.

Your attitude is everything when it comes to motivation. Try replacing negative thoughts with positive ones. One of my biggest challenges was to not be discouraged and allow the negativity to get the best of me. Be prepared to deal with difficulty and changes in plans or your path. Eliminate naysayers. Try not to overthink; it's alright not to know the answer at times. You also must NEVER allow fear to interrupt your motivation. The answers will come to you when you least expect them. Just keep moving; as NIKE's slogan says, "Just do it!" and as retired baseball player Wade Boggs said, "A positive attitude causes a chain reaction of positive thoughts, events, and outcomes. It is a catalyst and it sparks extraordinary results".

Each person is different and may have completely opposite feelings towards the same task. Some will hate it, others may love it. Why do you think this happens? It is simple. Some of us find ways to make any task interesting and fun to do! Take exercise, for example: visiting your local gym daily for a half-hour workout sounds rather boring to many of us, especially me. Yet, many people love going! They like exercising not only because they realize the benefits behind it, but also simply because it's fun! At a certain time in their daily schedule, they find going to the gym to be the best thing to do, simply because nothing else will fit their time and lifestyle so perfectly. I encourage you to try to live a healthy lifestyle. For example, I personally try to avoid products with large amounts of sugar. I attempt to create a schedule or a routine. Also, leave some room for changes in your plans, such as you will go to the gym at least three times a week, but not pick specific days. As long as you go, you're still sticking to a schedule or routine. You can have fun doing just about anything, depending on how you look at it! Just look for ways of having fun and you will find them! I allow myself a small award if I achieve my weekly gym goal and a larger reward if I overachieve my weekly gym goal. Try having a morning and evening routine for maximum results.

Not every task may seem beneficial at first, but if you take a few moments to analyze it, you can easily spot something good. For example, as a student, I used to believe studying wasn't a necessary task. However, after several disappointing grades, I realized I needed to find an effective yet fun way to study. Select a day and time where your schedule is usually free; an hour is suggested. At the end of the study session quiz yourself and treat yourself to something yummy! I love frozen yogurt.

We also have many tasks which do not require any reasoning at all; we have been doing them for so long that they feel natural. If you are ever stuck with tasks you hate and there seems to be no motivation to complete it, find good reasons to complete those tasks. The reasons may not be obvious, but stay at it until you see some. This will bring your motivation back and will help you finish the task. Give it a try!

I have found that utilizing your resources is a great way to stay motivated. My parents would not settle for me failing, which sparked a passion for my success. During my college years, I took advantage of all the resources the university provided, from tutors to study labs. These resources helped me drastically improve my academic grades and increase my love for learning. Utilize the school's local resources such as counselors, advisors, and your instructors. In addition, many communities have resources such as community agencies and social service providers to help individuals deal with more personal issues.

When things get tough, you must get tougher. Someone once said, "A smooth sea never made a skilled sailor." Always remember that to stay motivated. Remembering Thomas Edison's words of wisdom and recognizing the progress you have made thus far will help you stay motivated: "Our greatest weakness lies in giving up. The most certain way to succeed is always to try just one more time." Your progress can be measured by the completion of your short-term or long-term goals. All my life, my parents told me to "Dream big." They motivated me to be great and to aim for perfection and to never settle for anything less than average. I ask the same of you right now. As a society, we think of failure as a horrible thing, but without failure, there's no success; don't let failure rob you of your motivation. I also have struggled to overcome the fear of failure in order to live a happy life, and found the key to be "not letting the perfect be the enemy of the good." Is aiming for perfection healthy?

I believe we are all so much better than we are led to believe. It is up to us to recognize our strengths. American author and pastor, John C. Maxwell, said; "Fail early, fail often, but always fail forward." I couldn't agree more with this statement. We can no longer just go with the flow because our willpower and confidence have been depleted. We cannot just go along, because of the stories we've heard of the others who have failed. Always stay strong, because things will get better. It may be stormy

now, but rain doesn't last forever. I encourage you to
remain positive and stay motivated through it all.

Step Four: Be Yourself!

As we come to the fourth step, we must remember a few things. We will begin with a quote from the late and great Mother Teresa who said, "These are the few ways we can practice humility: To speak as little as possible of one's self. To mind one's own business. Not to want to manage other people's affairs. To avoid curiosity. To accept contradictions and correction cheerfully. To pass over the mistakes of others. To accept insults and injuries. To accept being slighted, forgotten and disliked. To be kind and gentle even under provocation. Never to stand on one's dignity. To choose always the hardest." It's time to just be you!

Never take life for granted. You must always remember life is too short to be mean. Smile more in your day, say hello to a stranger, and be more loving to one another. No one is in charge of your happiness except you.

You are the star of your own movie. Although it is okay to be proud of who you are, I also invite and encourage you to be a humble soul. Be united with each other. People who practice humility tend to reflect inward, but also focus their energy on other people. Throughout our entire life, we will establish many relationships, from childhood friends, to classmates, to co-workers, to love interests. We need to treat others how we would like to be treated. Is a one-sided relationship effective? No. Establish communication and trust. Help each other. Admit when you are wrong and be sympathetic. A relationship can be a magical experience. Try to work on relationships through being more accepting and compassionate. If you have broken relationships, fix them. Don't allow them to stay damaged. Learn to forgive. I can recount several times my "friends" have wronged me. However, I had to be strong to move past these troubles of life. I had to make peace with the past, so it would not impact my future. Get over the past and embrace the future. Take responsibility for everything that happens to you and move on.

Try to begin your day with a prayer, or by reciting some motivational words. In AA (Alcoholics Anonymous), they say a prayer daily, called The Serenity Prayer: "God grant me the serenity to accept the things I cannot change; courage to change the things I can; and wisdom to know the difference." I recite this prayer to myself often. Although I'm not a recovering alcoholic, it still holds meaning for me.

Life is full of loss. But, in a sense, real happiness would not be possible without it. It helps us appreciate and savor the things that really matter. It helps us grow. It can help us help others grow. "Closure" is a word for people who have never really suffered; in reality there is no such thing. Just try to "manage" your loss. Put it in perspective.

You will always have some regret and doubt about your loss. You may always second guess yourself; forgive.

As a college or high school student you are still early in your life and educational career; your years are yet to come. You will be presented with various problems and issues that will eventually be only memories

As a child, I remember going to Blockbuster Video, a weekly occurrence, sometimes even twice a weekend. I am often reminded by the label on the Blockbuster VHS rental which stated, "Be kind; please rewind." I will never forget that. This label will forever remind me to take a minute to rewind (or slow down); be kind in life. Every day, I use the manners I was taught as a young child: I greet people, I smile at people, I open doors for people, and I help people. My late grandmother Helen used to say, "You catch more flies with honey than vinegar." This is how I look at most aspects of life: to be sweet rather than bitter.

Working in the educational systems, and more specifically in high school settings, I observe many teenage interactions on a daily basis. The general outcomes seem to be if you aren't the kid with the most money and nicest clothes, you are practically invisible with nothing to offer. We live in an era where we thrive off pride and shun humility.

Ultimately, we ask ourselves a multitude of big life questions like, Why are we so miserable? Why do we have everything, yet nothing? What do we need to feel plentiful? I find myself pondering these thoughts quite often. Why does a society go about their time following the next man's dream, yet never decide to live their own lives? Day to day, we often see similar personalities and zero originality. This needs to change. We need to go out and be original. Live our own lives. Many people fall into categories of a certain type; I do not. I am an eclectic individual. This is what I would like to help you accomplish. Actress Bernadette Peters said, "You've gotta be original because if you're like someone else, what do they need you for?"

As a small child, my dad would often call me Buddha. I never knew why until one day as an adult, I asked. My dad replied, "Because as a baby you were small and round like him". My face puzzled. I said, "That's it?" There had to be more. As an adult, I researched Buddha. Buddha was "The Awakened One". He was an individual who taught people how to live a happy and peaceful life. This is exactly how I feel as a counselor and educator. Was this a premonition from my dad? Did he always know? Did my dad want me to follow the teachings of Buddha? Make peace, live your life, and be kind.

Step Five: Have Fun, Be Happy!

In my eyes, step five is one of the most essential. A student of mine once told me, "YOLO" (You Only Live Once), and he was right! Life is much too short to not enjoy the moment. Although this slogan (YOLO) may often be associated with performing a risky task, life is one-of-a-kind and should never be taken lightly. In my lifetime, I have seen many people come and go through death and changes in life's path. Happiness is healthy (and contagious)! Take the time to enjoy the present, your life, and be happy. Lucius Annaeus Seneca, a Roman Stoic philosopher (try saying that title five times fast) once said, "True happiness is... to enjoy the present, without anxious dependence upon the future". I want you to be happy.

Imagine this: a driver cuts you off, or your friend never texted you back. Both are events of everyday life that may tend to make you unhappy. Try to change your habits, and your approach in life. Instead of flipping the driver the bird, turn on relaxing music or just smile. Everyone can find a reason to be offended on a steady basis. So what caused you to be offended? You assigned bad intent to these otherwise harmless actions. You took it as a personal affront, a slap in the face. Happy people do not do this. They don't take things personally. They don't ascribe intent to the unintentional actions of others. My parents always wanted me to be happy. Unhappiness and stress are not allowed! (Write that on your refrigerator post it note).

As fast-paced and competitive as this world is, the average person experiences stress and exhaustion every day. Too much stress is harmful to your physical, emotional, and mental health. Although it is important to perform well and keep up with life's demands, take a break and see what else life has to offer. Try a hobby such as exercising, art, or playing a sport. Experiment and explore a few of your interests. Find your niche. Don't be afraid to try something new. Take a risk! Give it a try! My hobbies include exercising, traveling, entertaining, and attending live performances. As a teenager and young child, my parents and I often traveled; I always had a passion and love for traveling. I made it a goal of mine to use all the modes of transportation, from trains to cruise ships and subways: a goal accomplished. Every year I try to plan some type of trip; my favorites include large cities with lots of art and entertainment. My next travel goal is to visit more locations outside of the country. There are so many great sites and adventures out there waiting for you. Multiple online discount travel sites can be extremely cheap. Try using travel sites with package deals. Go see the world! Enjoy the finer things in life such as theater, fine dining, or the arts. Many communities have music venues and art shows. Take a trip and relax. Tomorrow is not promised, so you should enjoy every minute of your life.

As a child, in addition to traveling, my parents made sure I was involved at home, having fun and being active. I was a boy scout, active in the church community, and also very involved in my high school and community activities. There are healthy benefits to having fun. The positivity that comes from smiling, laughing, and having fun can even help you live longer. A group of American psychologists discovered that positive thinkers live 7.5 years longer than pessimists (those who think negatively). According to the study, "constant worrying puts a burden on the heart, increasing one's chances of giving in to the negative effects of stress" (Mayo Clinic). Dr. Becca Levy of Yale University says, "Having an optimistic attitude towards aging is better than having low blood pressure and cholesterol levels. So go ahead! Have fun! Take advantage of the health benefits of laughter and smiling. Laughter is simply the best medicine. 'A cheerful heart is good medicine.'" (PS 17:22).

Step Six: Count Your Blessings

One of the fondest lessons my parents taught me was not to take life for granted. My parents being religious and spiritual often informed me to appreciate everything I have in life and to be grateful. It truly dawned on me as one afternoon I walked the streets of New York City and observed individuals lying in corners. They called these locations home. You have to count your blessings each and every day. Appreciate what your life has presented you with, the privileges you have, and rewards you have reaped. Many people across the world do not have food, shelter, or many other necessities. One cold winter afternoon, I met a homeless man panhandling for change outside of a local drug store. My heart broke only imagining the challenges he was faced with day to day. Although I didn't have any change to spare, I brought him to the grocery store and purchased a meal for him. In the weeks to come, I continued to provide support, as I knew this was someone in need.

Growing up, I was lucky to have married parents. I lived in a wonderful home, traveled often, had food on the table, and attended college. Many people often are unable to access possessions in life we may take for granted, such as health care, running water, clean and healthy housing, and other luxuries.

On March 15, 2015, an acquaintance of mine lost his life in a car crash. I didn't know him too well, but as I waited in line at his wake, I looked around and saw how many people were present. I thought to myself, was he a good man? Was he a man who took life for granted? Did he accomplish all his goals? Was he happy? I hoped he was truly able to live the life he wanted. Sometimes individuals do not appreciate the life they have and take life as though it is owed to them. People need to stop often, relax, and enjoy life.

Put down the electronics! Look at the beautiful nature around you. Engage in social activities with your friends and loved ones. Go hiking, or join a social organization or charity. Get outside; it's a great day. We only have one life to live. Don't compare your life to others, and do not judge them. You have no idea what their life is about. My mother is a strong believer that *tomorrow is not a given;* it is a hope. Tragedy can touch us at a moment's notice; sometimes it does. And the tragedy is not only simply about the loss of life; sometimes it can be about the loss of what was. We have all suffered a loss of some sort or another: a friendship is severed; a beloved one becomes suddenly ill; a job is lost; a moment changes everything. While a loss can penetrate our being, it doesn't have to define our every step. Or if it does, make it count for good.

At all times you must take care of your body and mind. We also have to remember one thing: in the words of martial artist Bruce Lee, "I want you to always be yourself, express yourself, have faith in yourself, do not go out and look for a successful personality and duplicate it". Don't over think! Live your life!

Although there are many definitions of success, you have to provide your own definition. Is it the college degree you worked so hard for? Is it the spouse and kids you longed for? Or is it simply a one-bedroom apartment which you pay rent for? Your success is measured by your own accomplishments.

The steps my parents instilled in me have helped me succeed. I measure my success by how I give back to others and how happy I am in my life. I feel I have completed all my steps and you can too.

As my life continues, I still live by the lessons and values my parents have instilled in me. I use these same lessons to inspire my students, my peers, and colleagues on a daily basis. I cannot encourage you enough to remember the six steps in your day to day activities. We all strive to be perfect, yet no one is. We cannot allow anyone to put pressure on us. I leave you with these two words: Live Boldly. Every single time you are offered a choice that involves greater risk, take it. You will lose on many of them, but when you add them up at the end of your life you'll be glad you did. Making mistakes is human, and we need to allow ourselves and others to not be perfect; try your best and go forward! The world is your oyster; live it up! Find your passion and go for it! Impossible is nothing, live strong! Make peace with yourself. I hope you find your

purpose in life!

Thanks for listening!

Shelby

Avalee

all the Best!

To you

Reflection

If I could close with one final poem to summarize a way to live your life, this would be it:

"All I Really Need To Know I Learned In Kindergarten"

By Robert Fulghum

Most of what I really need
to know about how to live
And what to do and how to be
I learned in kindergarten.
Wisdom was not at the top
of the graduate school mountain,
but there in the sandpile at Sunday school.

These are the things I learned:

Share everything.
Play fair.
Don't hit people.
Put things back where you found them.
Clean up your own mess.
Don't take things that aren't yours.
Say you're sorry when you hurt somebody.
Wash your hands before you eat.
Flush.
Warm cookies and cold milk are good for you.
Live a balanced life -
Learn some and think some

and draw and paint and sing and dance
and play and work every day some.
Take a nap every afternoon.
When you go out into the world,
Watch out for traffic,
Hold hands and stick together.
Be aware of wonder.

Resources:

Mayo Clinic Staff, *Stress Management*, Mayo Clinic, http://www.mayoclinic.org (accessed May 6, 2014).

Francesca Zapanta, *Happiness is Healthy: the Benefits of Having Fun.* April 07, 2010. Female Network, http://www.femalenetwork.com (accessed May 6, 2014).

The Psychology of Fun Play and Engagement, January 24, 2014. The James Maples Organization, http://www.jamesmapes.com (accessed May 6, 2014)

Andy Simmons, *Hilarious Jokes from the Guys Who Make America Laugh.* Joke by Harry Nelson. Reader's Digest. http://www.rd.com (accessed May 6, 2014).

Author, N. (2014, April 17). Chapter 2: Public Views on the Value of Education | Pew Research Center. Retrieved from: http://www.pewsocialtrends.org/2014/02/11/chapter-2-public-views-on-the-value-of-education/

Help Your Students Earn A's by Not Focusing on Grades. (n.d.). Retrieved from https://www.insidehighered.com/news/2017/08/01/research-suggests-students-may-make-more-academic-progress-focusing-task-oriented

About the Author

Mr. Shelby C. Davis is a counselor in the public school system and a college professor. He received his Masters in Counseling and Higher Education from the University of Bridgeport. Mr. Shelby C. Davis also is a graduate of Western Connecticut State University (Go Colonials!) with a Bachelor of Arts in Social Work. A true Connecticut native, in his spare time, he enjoys volunteering, spending time with his dog Murphy, acting and directing in theatrical arts, exercising (no pain no gain) and traveling (viva la Mexico). Shelby also mentors individuals in his community and is a vibrant educator of diversity-related issues, theater, and career building.

Made in the USA
Middletown, DE
02 February 2019